ORIGAMI
for children

ORIGAMI
for children

35 easy-to-follow step-by-step projects

MARI ONO AND ROSHIN ONO

CICO BOOKS

LONDON NEW YORK

Published in 2008 by CICO Books
an imprint of Ryland Peters & Small
519 Broadway, 5th Floor, New York, NY 10012

www.cicobooks.co.uk

10 9 8 7 6 5 4 3 2

A CIP catalog record for this book is available
from the Library of Congress

ISBN-13: 978 1 906094 38 6
ISBN-10: 1 906094 38 1

Printed in China

Editor: Robin Gurdon
Designer: Claire Legemah
Step Photography: Debbie Patterson
Style Photography: Carolyn Barber
Stylist: Rose Hammick

Contents

INTRODUCTION

Origami, the art of folding paper, has long been a traditional activity for Japanese children. Most learn the techniques from their parents and grandparents, or perhaps their kindergarten teacher, but however they learn they all soon become absorbed in the magic of origami.

This book will show you how to fold classic origami designs using Japanese *origami* (paper), both with beautiful, traditional *chiyogami* motifs and in modern designs. Although origami is over 100 years old, exciting designs and papers continue to be developed. This book introduces the latest of both as well as the traditional techniques.

Your children may feel that some origami techniques are difficult but this will only be temporary. As they discover other models using similar techniques they will use their experience to improve their skills. It will soon become clear that what at first seems complicatesd, is just a combination of basic techniques.

At the origami workshops I have held, many participating children were surprised by origami, saying it is "just like a magic!" It is also highly appreciated by parents because, unlike electronic games, it helps develop concentration and gives children a feeling of accomplishment.

Another great advantage of origami is the ability for you and your children to enjoy practicing it anywhere you can fold a piece of paper. Allow yourselves to relax with friends as a single piece of paper transforms itself into a balloon, animal, or airplane in front of your eyes.

In this book I have introduced a series of toys made using Japanese traditional designs, a range of practical items that are useful for a children's party, and a number of models of a more modern design, such as a zebra, a giraffe, plus some cakes and other tasty foods. Also, there are the boats, airplanes, and rockets, which all boys love.

Now it's time to experience an exciting world filled with magical origami!

PAPER

The word *origami* actually has two meanings in Japanese: it is both the act of folding paper to make models or objects, and the particular type of square paper used itself. To "fold" in Japanese is *ori* while the general translation of "paper" is *kami*, and when joined together the two become *origami*—any type of paper that can be folded.

You can try folding paper of almost any kind—from office paper to wrapping paper—though tissue-paper is unsuitable because of its lack of strength. You can purchase all types of Japanese *origami* papers from the suppliers listed on page 126. Here is a selection of some of the origami papers I have used in this book.

Right: The six patterns shown here are all examples of *chiyogami*, paper decorated with brightly colored, woodblock-printed patterns. Originating in 1700 in the ancient capital of Japan, Kyoto, the high-quality pattern designs of *chiyogami* were always used by the upper classes; *chiyogami* is now recognized across the world for its quality and patterns. I used modern *chiyogami* in the projects to make the *Kabuto*—Samurai Helmet (page 30) and the *San-pou*—Candy Box (page 83).

Left: Modern printing techniques have made it possible to print any pattern on *origami*. Some of the most famous patterned *origami* are the cute and colorful floral patterns that replicate the papers of ancient Japan. Available in every design and color combination, I have used floral paper for many of the projects including the *Ie*—House (page 20) and *Cop-shiki*—Coaster (page 89).

Right: *Origami* also comes in more modern designs. The paper shown here is called harmony *origami*, which uses geometric patterns and the beautiful effects of color gradation to create striking papers. The appealing designs have brought an up-to-date originality to *origami*, confirming its continued importance. I used the harmony *origami* for many of the projects in this book including the *Hoshi*—Star (page 37) and *Hikouki*—Airplane (page 118).

Opposite: Some of the simplest papers are the prettiest, and using *origami* of the same design in different color combinations can be a great way of making sets of a similar design. I used paper like this for the *Hana Kago*—Flower Basket (page 95) so that I could make a group of baskets that were all slightly different to each other.

INTRODUCTION

ORIGAMI ESSENTIAL ADVICE

1. Use a table. It sounds simple, but it is so effective.

2. Make sure your folds are accurate at the points. This is the key to achieving beautiful origami.

3. Make firm folds. This will help the origami to stay in place and give you a clean finish.

ARROWS

Fold
Fold the part of the paper shown in this direction

Folding direction
Fold the entire paper over in this direction

Open out
Open out and refold the paper in the direction shown

Change the position
Spin the paper 90° in the direction of the arrows

Change the position
Spin the paper through 180°

Turn over
Turn the paper over

Make a crease
Fold the paper in the direction of the arrow then open it out again

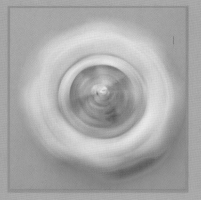

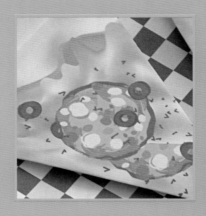

THE
projects

1 FUSEN BALLOON

This is one of the most magical of traditional origami models—a sheet of paper folds flat before being inflated with a single breath into a three-dimensional form to become a toy ball. This balloon will show you all the pleasure of origami-folding—it is simple to make and you can increase your enjoyment by making it with papers of different sizes and colors.

You will need
10 in (25cm) sheet of square paper

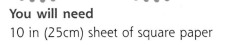

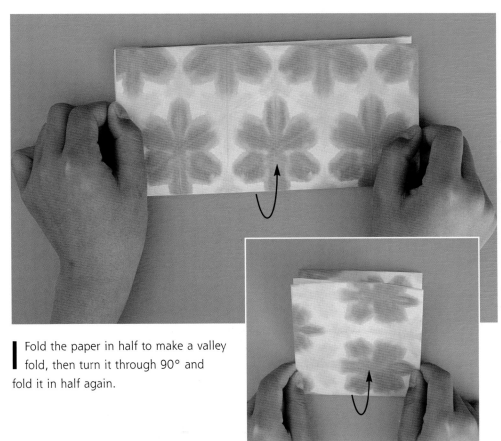

I Fold the paper in half to make a valley fold, then turn it through 90° and fold it in half again.

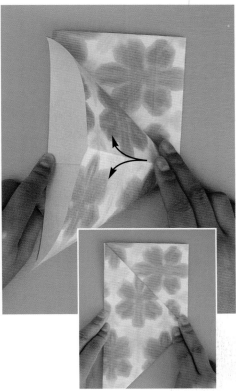

2 Open the upper pocket out into a triangle and press down.

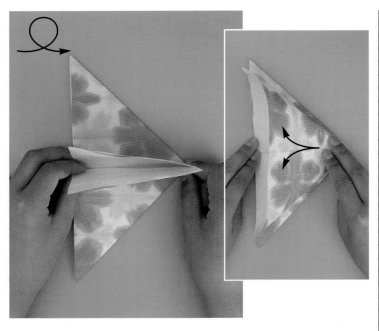

3 Turn the paper over and lift the square flap so that it can be opened out in the same way as in the previous step.

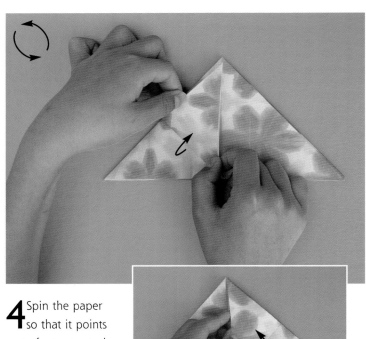

4 Spin the paper so that it points away from you and lift the left-hand corner, turning it up to the far point of the triangle. Repeat on the other side.

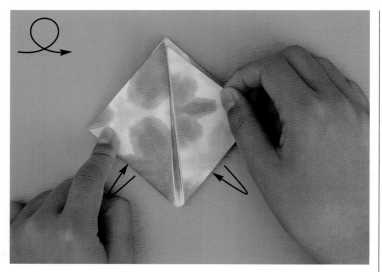

5 Turn the paper over and again turn the outer corners up to the top point, making a diamond shape.

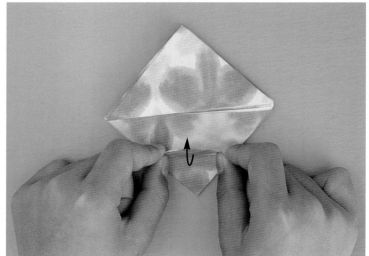

6 Spin the paper through 90° again and fold the top and bottom points in so that they meet in the center.

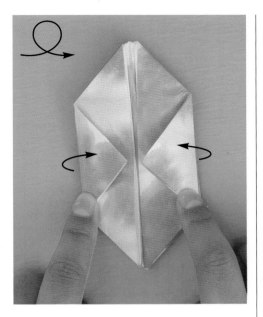

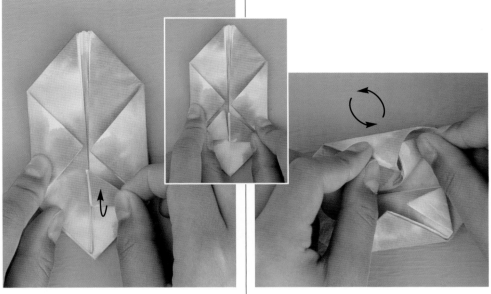

7 Turn the paper over and repeat on the other side.

8 Fold the lower tips of the top layer up toward the center so that the folded edge runs along the central triangle.

9 Spin the paper around 90°. Now fold the triangular-shaped flap you have just made along its bottom edge and, opening up the pocket in the center, tuck it inside.

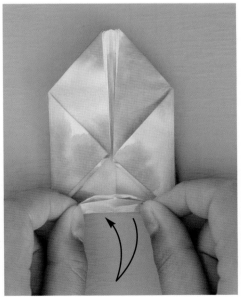

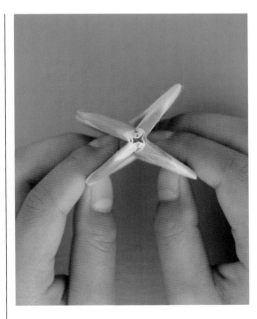

10 Repeat on the other flap before turning the paper over and repeating on the other side.

11 Fold up the bottom tip and score the fold before releasing. Repeat on the other side.

12 Open the flaps out into a cross shape and blow gently through the hole, inflating the balloon while easing out the creases.

2 IE HOUSE

You can make anything in *origami*: here a house is being created from a single sheet of flower-patterned paper. The design is extremely simple so you could also enjoy making it from square paper in any variety of colors and sizes. Why not make an entire paper town to play with!

You will need
6 in (15 cm) sheet of square paper

| Fold the paper in half to make a crease. Open it back out, turn the paper over, and spin it 90° before folding it in half again across the original crease.

2 Fold the top part of the paper in half so that the edge runs along the center crease.

3 Turn over, spin the paper through 90°, and fold in one side to the center followed by the other.

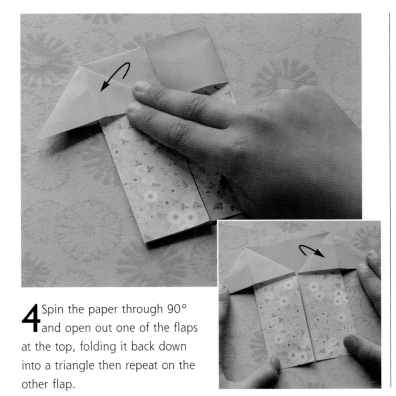

4 Spin the paper through 90° and open out one of the flaps at the top, folding it back down into a triangle then repeat on the other flap.

5 Make a firm crease by folding the bottom up to meet the triangle folds. Let it go to become the stand for the house.

3 **KOMA** SPINNING TOP

Origami is magic! Here, three pieces of paper are transformed into a spinning top. Although the steps look difficult at first, they are actually unexpectedly easy. Each of the three pieces of paper fits into the next until a beautifully-colored top has been created which spins around very smartly. By the time you have put the third piece in place, it has become a gorgeous spinning top.

You will need
3 sheets of 6 in (15 cm) square paper

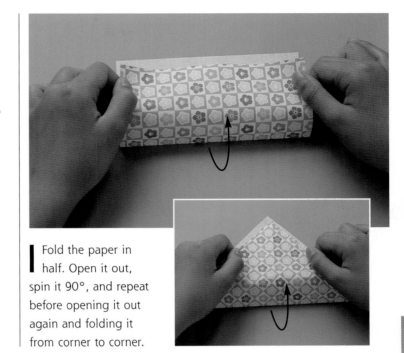

I Fold the paper in half. Open it out, spin it 90°, and repeat before opening it out again and folding it from corner to corner.

2 Fold all of the corners to meet in the center.

3 Repeat the first two steps with two other pieces of origami, making sure they are all the same size.

23

KOMA SPINNING TOP

4 Spin the paper through 45° and fold the corners into the center once again.

5 Repeat one more time, folding all the corners in to meet at the center.

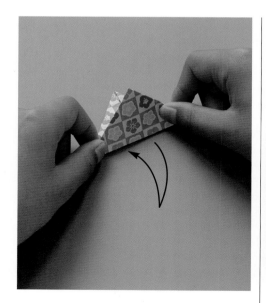

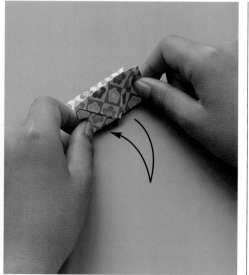

6 Turn the object over and fold it in half in both directions to make creases from corner to corner.

7 Next, turn the object over and fold it in half to make horizontal creases in both directions and open out.

8 Squeeze the paper at the corners, pressing it together to make a point.

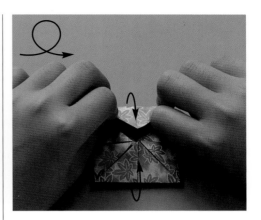

9 Take the second sheet, turn it over and fold the corners into the center.

10 Turn the paper over and fold the corners into the center.

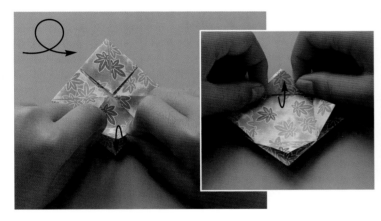

11 Turn the paper over again and fold back each of the four top flaps so that they touch the outer points.

12 Open one of the flaps on the second sheet and place one of the points of the first piece underneath, repeating around the object until it is firmly in position.

13 Now take the third sheet, open it out and fold both edges into the center.

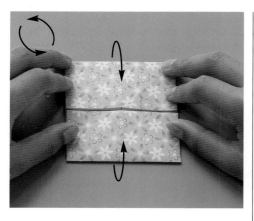

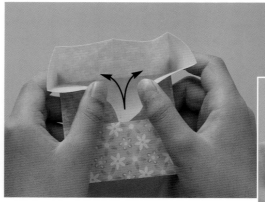

14 Spin the paper through 90° and fold both edges into the center to make the object into a square.

15 Turn back the far flap, opening out the folds to make triangles before pressing the paper flat again.

TOYS

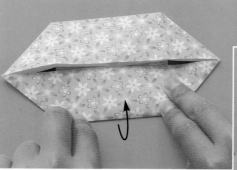

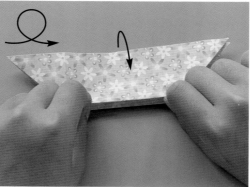

16 Repeat on the other side before turning the paper over and folding it in half toward you.

17 Fold the top left flap forward so that it points straight down.

18 Repeat, turn over, and fold forward the last two points.

19 Spin the paper 180°, pull open one flap and flatten it into a square then repeat on the other flap.

20 Turn the sheet over and repeat on the other flaps to make a rectangle.

21 Open the paper out into a square. On each of the four top flaps fold in the outer corners to meet in the middle, so that the edges run beside each other.

22 Fold each corner in, making small, equal triangles.

23 At each corner, open out the pair of flaps before folding them back over the long side of the triangles, flattening them into diamond shapes.

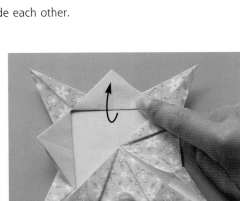

24 Fold back each of the four points that meet in the center to make the outline of a square.

25 Fold the long points back over the triangles toward the center.

26 Fit the first object into the third sheet, placing the corners under the flaps but on top of the folded diamonds.

PACMAN THE MUNCHER

Handed down from mother to child, there are many traditional origami models and this is one of the simplest. You put your fingers into the holes, and open and close *paku-paku*'s mouth in every different direction. You can also write a number and a word on the eight faces inside to make a fun game. Alternatively, place it upside down on a table to make a candy box filled with jelly beans for a party.

You will need
6 in (15 cm) sheet of square paper

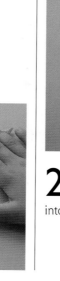

I Fold the paper from corner to corner, open out and repeat in the other direction.

2 Open out and fold each of the corners into the center.

3 Turn over and fold the corners into the center once again.

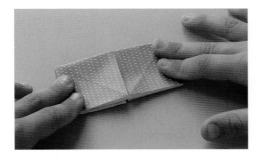

4 Fold the paper in half to make a rectangle.

5 Turn over and open out by placing your fingers underneath the flaps.

You will need
12 in (30 cm) sheet of *chiyogami*

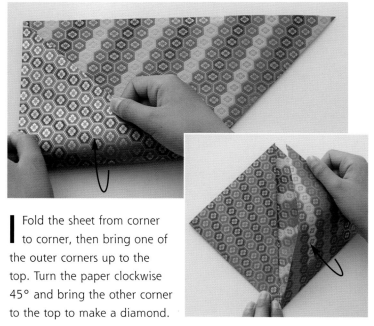

| Fold the sheet from corner to corner, then bring one of the outer corners up to the top. Turn the paper clockwise 45° and bring the other corner to the top to make a diamond.

5 KABUTO
SAMURAI HELMET

A *kabuto* is a Japanese *samurai* helmet from the Middle Ages. In Japan, the *samurai* helmet is recreated in miniature across the country every year on Children's Day, which celebrates the healthy growth and development of boys. The *kabuto* is often made from a sheet of newspaper for little children to wear. You can enjoy making a *kabuto* using brightly colored *chiyogami* paper.

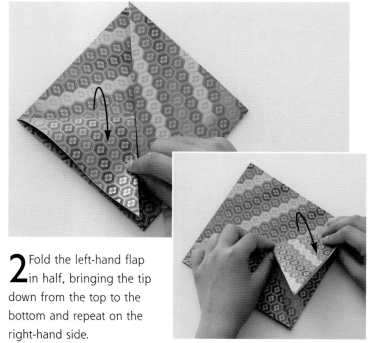

2 Fold the left-hand flap in half, bringing the tip down from the top to the bottom and repeat on the right-hand side.

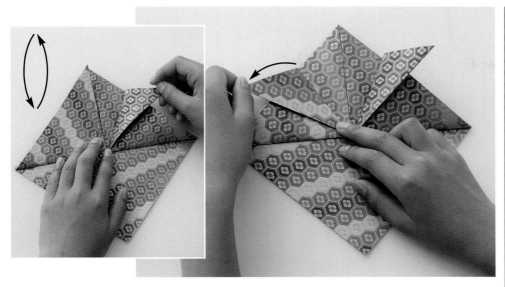

3 Spin the paper through 180° and turn down the top flap so that the outer edge runs down the center of the triangle, repeating on the other side.

4 Turn up the front of the bottom so that the tip is in line with the previous folds.

31

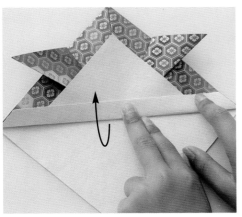

5 Fold up the remaining part of the bottom section along the center line.

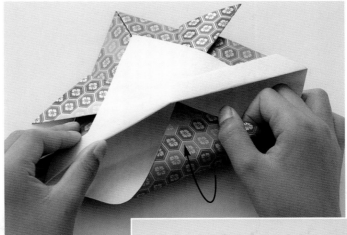

6 Fold the back forward to make a crease.

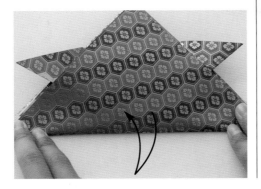

7 Fold the flap inside the helmet and squeeze the points together to open out the hat.

KABUTO SAMURAI HELMET

6 SHURIKEN NINJA KNIFE

In the history of Japan, a ninja was a specially trained warrior skilled in martial arts and spying. One of the weapons that a Japanese ninja used in the Middle Ages was the knife, which was thrown at an unsuspecting enemy. Although the real knife is very dangerous, a representation in origami is safe, fascinating to look at, and fun to make. When you combine two different colors of origami together, you can make this intriguing replica of a famous Japanese artifact.

You will need
2 sheets of 6 in (15 cm) metallic square paper

1 Cut two pieces of origami in half and use one of each color to make one *shuriken*.

2 Fold one piece of paper lengthwise and then fold it in half again, making a strong crease.

3 Turn over the corners at right angles so that the top edge now runs down the side of the object.

4 Turn over the top point across the object at a 90° angle to form a triangle whose base runs across the center crease.

5 Repeat with the bottom point, folding in the opposite direction.

6 Do the same folds on the second sheet, ensuring that the corners folded in step 3 are turned in the opposite directions.

7 Turn the paper over then fold the tips over to make the same finished shape as the first sheet.

8 Place the first paper on top of the second so that they sit at right angles to each other.

9 Turn over the points of the lower sheet and slip them into the folds of the upper sheet.

10 Turn the object over and slip the final two tips into the remaining pockets.

7 HOSHI STAR

Although making a star with one piece of origami paper is simple, it can be a little fiddly at first. Like all origami, you will find it becomes much easier with a little bit of practice. Use paper of various sizes and patterns to make a range of colorful decorations.

You will need
6 in (15 cm) sheet of square paper

1 Start by folding the paper from corner to corner then fold in half along its longest edge.

2 Turn the upper part of the top flap forward, folding along a line across the center of the paper.

3 Fold the remaining top part of the object down and across at an angle so that the long side runs across the center of the object.

4 Lift the object and fold the top half of the object back and underneath along the center line.

5 Half open the top part of the object and pull out the flap of paper inside, reversing it as you do so.

6 Flatten it at an angle to form the next point of the star, making new creases inside the object.

7 Make a small angled flap with the bottom left-hand corner of the top layer.

8 Lift up the last remaining flap, refolding it at an angle to match the point opposite. Reverse the small fold made in the previous step to keep it in place.

9 Press down to make the last point and turn the object over.

8 OU-KAN CROWN

A shiny crown makes a party hat with a difference. You could give a gold one to the birthday girl or boy and silver versions to all your friends. Exceptionally easy to make, this design combines identically folded sheets but requires no glue or tape. I used nine sheets here, but add as many as you need to encircle the head, or use a different-sized paper. When you or your friends are wearing this origami crown, you will feel like you are ruling the world!

You will need
9 sheets of 15 cm (6 in) metallic square paper

1 Prepare nine sheets of paper by folding them into quarters and opening them out to leave creases. Then fold the corners into the center to make the *zabuton*, or floor cushion, shape.

2 Turn the sheet over and fold the corner into the middle once again.

41

OU-KAN CROWN

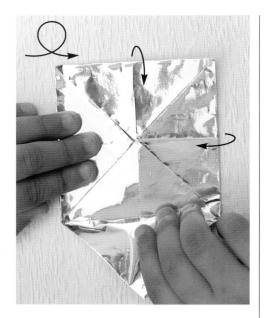

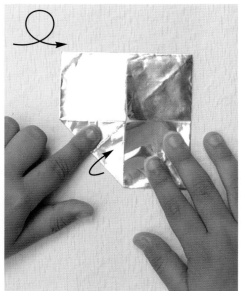

3 Turn the sheet back over and turn the corners into the middle.

4 Turn the sheet over and again fold the corners into the center.

5 Once again, turn the sheet over and open the flaps by placing your fingers inside and pulling the paper flat. Do this to three of the four flaps.

6 When you have made all nine sections of the crown, join them together by slotting one square arm inside another. When all nine are connected close the circle by joining the two remaining ends.

9 HAATO HEART

This heart is made from a square sheet of origami paper cut into a rectangle. I made it with beautiful gradated origami paper. This paper heart is great for a birthday card or Valentine's Day card, or even as a decoration for a wedding party. In addition, you can make it look like petals of a flower if you fix together five or six separate pieces made from small papers.

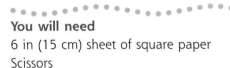

You will need
6 in (15 cm) sheet of square paper
Scissors

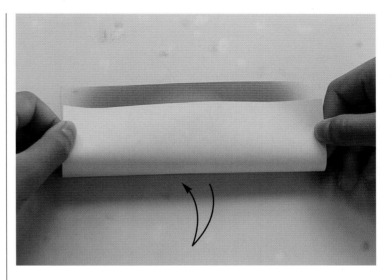

| Cut the sheet of origami into a rectangle and fold it in half to make a crease.

2 Open the paper back out, turn it over, and fold one edge into the center.

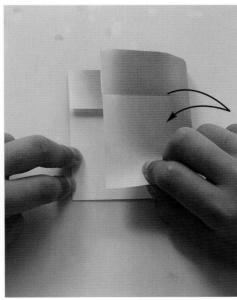

3 Fold the paper in half crosswise to make a crease.

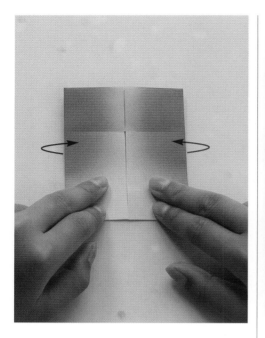

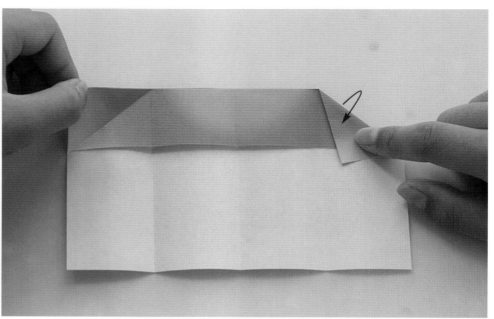

4 Open out and fold both sides into the center, meeting along the crease made in the previous step.

5 Open out the paper again and turn down the top corners at an angle, along a line from the top of the outer crease to the corner of the folded section.

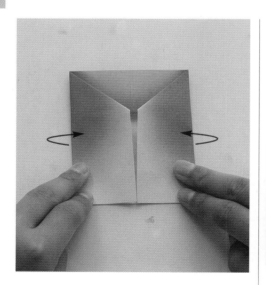

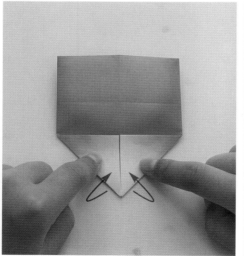

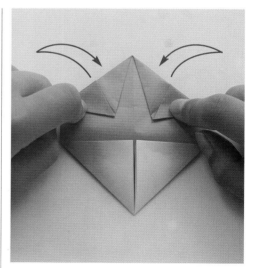

6 Fold both sides back into the center.

7 Turn the paper over and fold the bottom corners across to the center line.

8 Fold down the top corners at an angle to make a pair of creases.

9 Fold back the top corners and fold forward the top of the paper.

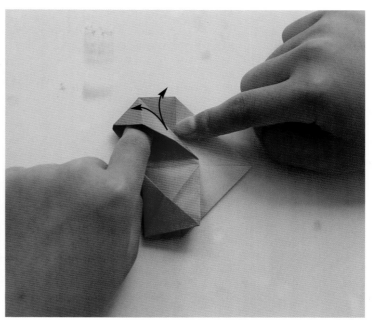

10 Spin the paper counterclockwise 90° and open out the top pocket, pressing the sheet flat again.

11 To finish, push open the other flap and then turn the object over.

10 **NEKUTAI**
NECK TIE

Use traditional *chiyogami* in a tie-dyed fabric pattern to make a tie as a card for Father's Day or as part of your teddy bear's wardrobe. Alternatively, create a life-size tie with a sheet of paper 12 in (30 cm) square.

You will need
7 in (18 cm) sheet of *chiyogami*

I Fold the paper from corner to corner.

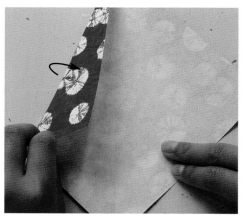

2 Open out the paper and spin it 90° so that the crease is vertical. Fold the corners into the center, running the edges down the center line.

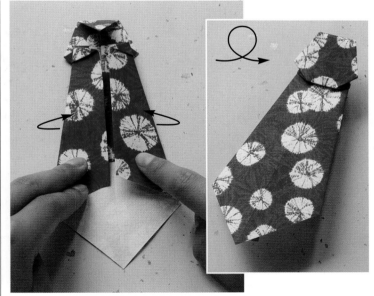

3 Turn the paper over and fold the tip forward so that it sits in line with the side points and make a crease.

4 Fold the tip back up, one-fifth of the way down from the top fold.

5 Make small folds on both sides of the long tip and push them underneath the fold made in the previous step.

6 Turn the object over and bend the tip back, halfway down its length, so that it falls on top of the main part of the object.

7 To finish, fold both sides in so that their edges meet at, and run down, the center line then turn the object over.

NEKUTAI NECK TIE

11 **ORUGAN** ORGAN

This organ design is one of the traditional origami techniques passed down by word of mouth from generation to generation. As the technique is very simple, this project is an ideal way to learn the basics of origami—for example, how to take out a crease and open a pocket. For an added effect, I made the organ here using modern origami paper with a big check pattern.

You will need

6 in (15 cm) sheet of square paper

I Starting with the colored side down, fold the sheet in half and then into quarters.

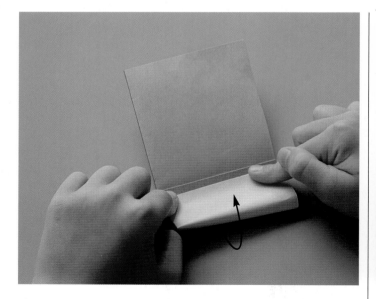

2 Open out the last fold and bring both edges to meet in the center.

3 Open out the sides again, making triangle folds at the top.

ORIGAMI FUN

50

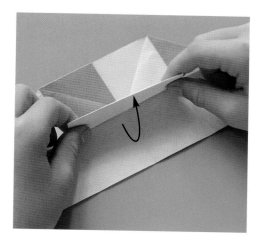

4 Fold the central flap up to the base of the triangles and fold again along the triangles to make the keyboard.

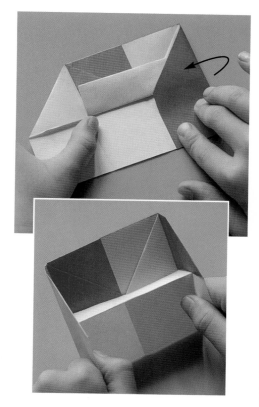

5 Turn in the corners and let the object open out so that it sits naturally. Finally draw the black keys on to the keyboard.

12 ENNPITSU PENCIL

Cutting a piece of bright origami into a long, thin rectangle makes a colored pencil—and paper of any kind or size will work just as well as origami paper. It's perfect as a bookmark, or have fun decorating your school classroom with lots of origami pencils.

You will need
6 in (15 cm) sheet of square paper
Scissors

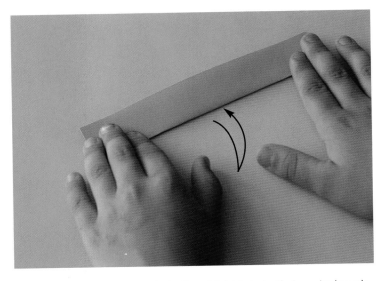

I Cut a sheet of origami in half and fold it in half along its length to make a crease.

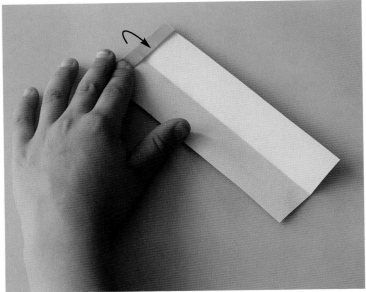

2 Open out the paper and turn over one end approximately ¹/₂ in (1 cm).

3 Turn the paper over and fold back the corners of the end worked on in the previous step to meet at the center crease.

4 Turn over the folded edges again, placing the angled edges together along the center line.

5 Turn the paper over and fold the flat end up so that ends up about ³/₄ in (2 cm) from the pointed end.

6 To finish, fold back both sides, hiding them under the object. Tuck one side into the pocket of the other so they are secure.

13 **KINGYO** GOLDFISH

This beautiful waterdrop-pattern origami makes a goldfish that looks like it's swimming through dappled water. The kingyo is one of origami's most magical designs from ancient times as, in the last step, it turns into a goldfish. It differs to many projects as you need to use scissors to finish it off, so make sure there is an adult around to help.

You will need
6 in (15 cm) sheet of square paper
Scissors

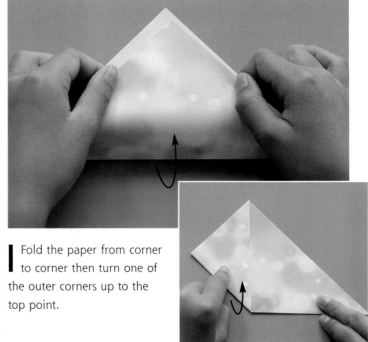

1 Fold the paper from corner to corner then turn one of the outer corners up to the top point.

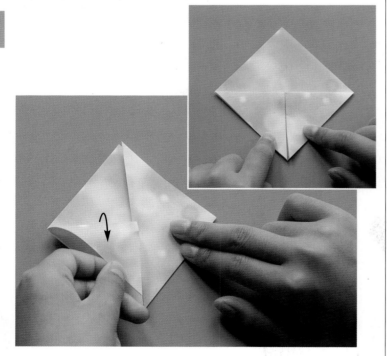

2 Repeat on the other corner then turn the top flaps down to the bottom point.

3 Spin the paper 180° and turn the folded tips down and across at a 45° angle.

54

ANIMALS

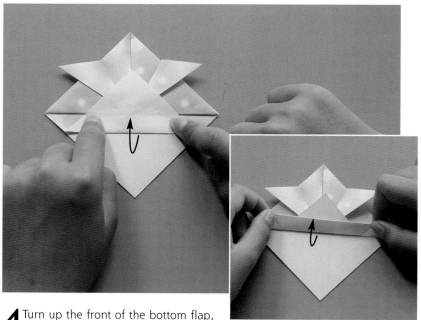

4 Turn up the front of the bottom flap, with the fold about ¹/₂ in (1 cm) from the middle of the object, then turn the fold back on itself along the center line.

5 Pick up the paper, turn it 90° and use a small pair of scissors to cut ³/₄ in (1.5 cm) slits through the single layer of paper along the center line.

6 Fold the single layer of paper left back behind the object.

7 Placing your fingers inside, pull open the object and flatten it down in the opposite direction.

8 Turn over the left-hand point to make a ½-in (1-cm) wide flap.

9 Let go of the flap and fold it back on itself, ending up inside the object.

10 Pick up the object and fold out the flap on the left to make the tail.

11 Finish by flattening out the tail so that it lies flush with the rest of the goldfish.

14 **INU** DOG

Making a lovely, large-eared dog is extremely simple. You can use large pieces of paper and then turn them into masks to wear and play with. When you have folded the face, draw on the dog's features and whiskers. Don't worry about accuracy; any face will give your dog character. Try different colored paper for different breeds.

You will need
6 in (15 cm) sheet of square paper
Marker pen or stick-on craft eyes

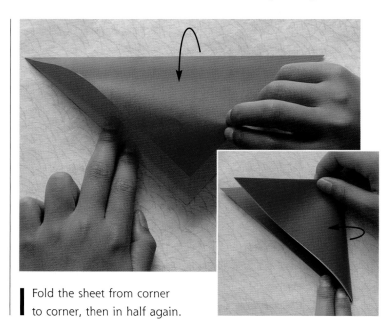

1 Fold the sheet from corner to corner, then in half again.

2 Open out the last fold and turn down the corners to make the ears.

3 Turn the object over and fold the top forward to make a flat edge.

4 Turn the object back over and fold up the front sheet of the bottom flap before turning the tip of the folded flap back over.

58

ANIMALS

5 Fold up the back flap and tuck it inside the object. Draw or add the eyes.

15 **PENGIN** PENGUIN

As this design is so easy to make, I decided to create a whole family of penguins. Although the design of the penguin is very simple, do take care with your folds to ensure that it can balance. Make enough models so that you can play with your own colony of lovely penguins.

You will need
6 in (15 cm) sheet of square paper

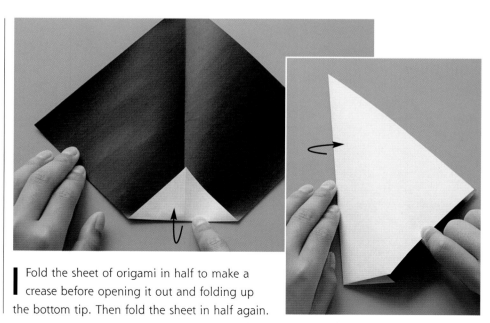

Fold the sheet of origami in half to make a crease before opening it out and folding up the bottom tip. Then fold the sheet in half again.

2 Turn back the upper sheet at an angle, then turn the object over and repeat.

3 Turn the long tip over at an angle across the straight edge to make the crease for the penguin's neck.

4 Open out the object and fold the tip back on itself to make the head, reversing the creases made in the previous step.

5 To finish, flatten the head so that it surrounds the top of the penguin.

16 NEKO CAT

This origami cat is a design that everyone can easily make. Each cat will become a real character just as soon as you draw on a pair of eyes, a nose, and set of whiskers using a marker pen. The paper I have used here is traditional Japanese hand-made *washi*, but any square paper will work just as well.

You will need
6 in (15 cm) sheet of traditional Japanese *washi* square paper
Marker pen

1 Fold over the paper from corner to corner, open it out and fold between the other corners.

2 Turn back the top of the triangle, making a fold about ³/₄ in (2 cm) from the tip.

3 Fold up the right-hand corner from the center crease at an angle so that it just covers the triangle made in the previous step.

ANIMALS

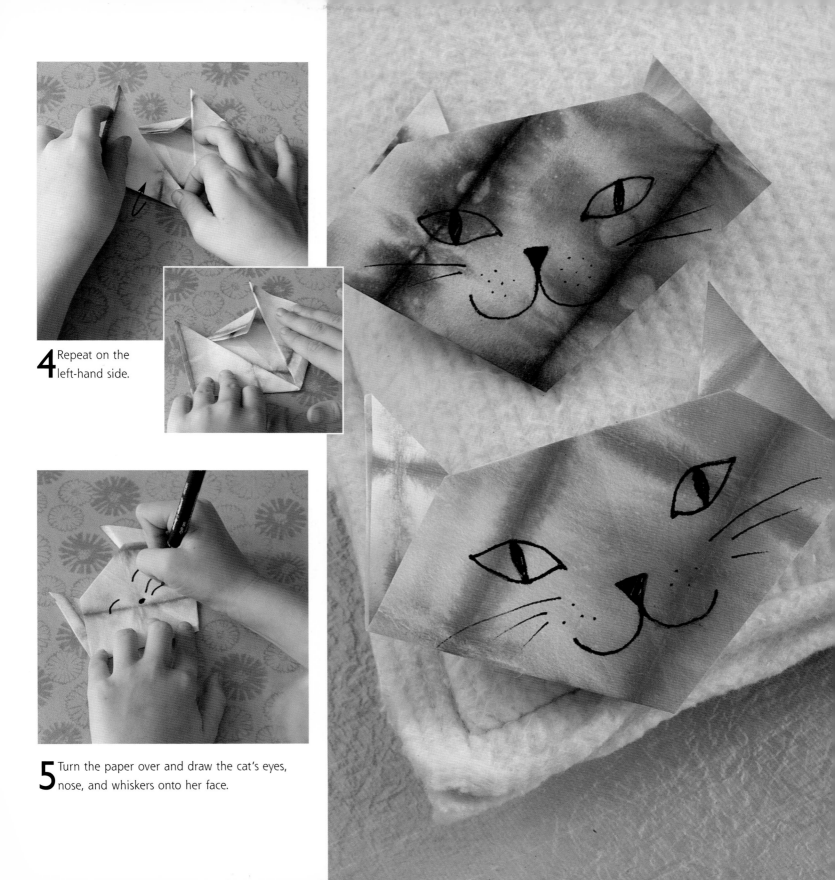

4 Repeat on the left-hand side.

5 Turn the paper over and draw the cat's eyes, nose, and whiskers onto her face.

17 SHIMA-UNA ZEBRA

The zebra is the one of the more complicated animals to make. Like many designs, some steps match other objects—here, the first stages resemble the techniques used for the steps for the house—so use your knowledge of other origami models to guide you.

You will need
2 sheets of 6 in (15 cm) square striped paper
Paper glue

I Fold the first sheet of paper in half.

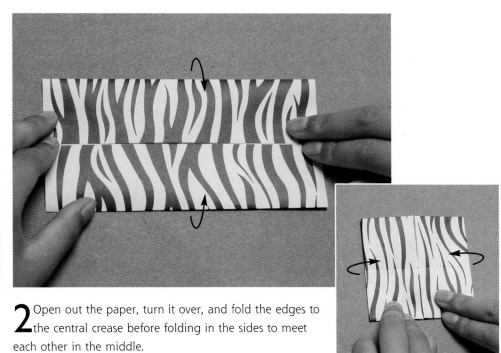

2 Open out the paper, turn it over, and fold the edges to the central crease before folding in the sides to meet each other in the middle.

3 Open out and push out the ends to make triangles.

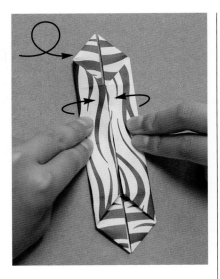

4 Turn over and fold both the long side edges into the center.

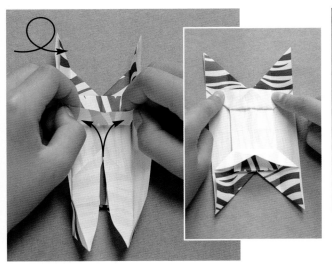

5 Turn over and open both flaps, pushing down one end before repeating at the other end.

6 Fold the object in half.

7 Fold each leg in half, turning the flaps along a line from the tip up to the center of the object.

8 Turn over and repeat, then turn over one corner of the back to make the zebra's tail.

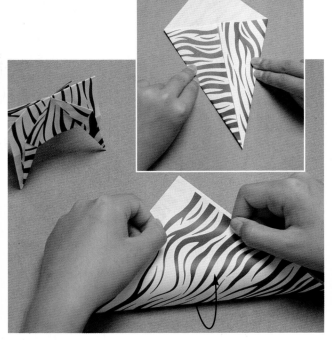

9 Take the second sheet and fold it from corner to corner then unfold it and turn both sides in so that the edges meet along the center crease.

10 Fold the paper in half, turning the bottom tip back underneath so that the tips meet.

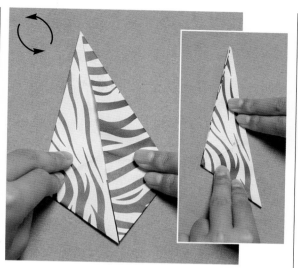

11 Spin the object through 90°, lift a flap and push it back down so that the edge runs down the center line.

12 Repeat on the other side to make a long diamond shape then fold the object in half.

13 Make an angled fold line to form the neck then open the object out slightly and turn the head over along the fold line.

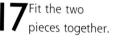

67

16 Fold half of the neck flap over to make the mane and repeat on the other side.

17 Fit the two pieces together.

SHIMA-UNA ZEBRA

14 Fold over the remaining tip and press it down before opening up the neck and folding the tip back inside.

15 Fold the nose back at an angle, then open out the head and fold the tip back inside.

18 **KIRINN** GIRAFFE

Modern *origami* is available in endless patterns and this one, replicating the coat of a giraffe, is ideal for making a model of the animal. Use one sheet of paper to make the neck and head, and a second for the legs and body, joining them together at the end. You could make a range of different animals and end up with a zoo of your own.

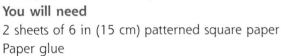

You will need
2 sheets of 6 in (15 cm) patterned square paper
Paper glue

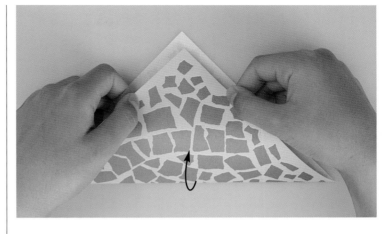

I Use the first sheet of paper to make the neck and head of the giraffe. Start by folding it in half.

2 Turn the paper through 90° and open out. Fold the outer points in toward the center so that the edges run down the crease. Turn each side over again to make these folded edges run down the center crease.

3 Turn up the bottom point, making a horizontal fold between the end points of the folded sides.

4 Fold the whole sheet in half along the central crease, making a valley fold.

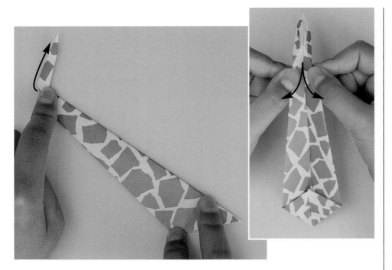

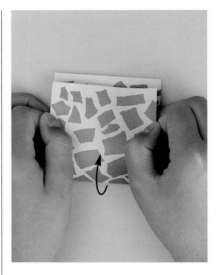

5 Make the head with an inside fold: first turn the end tip across the neck and make an angled crease. Next, open out the neck and push the tip away from you so that the head turns on itself along this, reversing the direction of original crease as it encloses the neck.

6 Give the head a snub nose with another inside fold, turning the tip right back underneath and inside the head.

7 Take the second sheet of paper, fold it in half, and then in half again to make a crease.

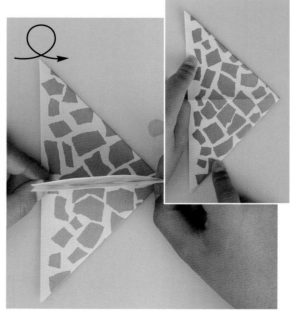

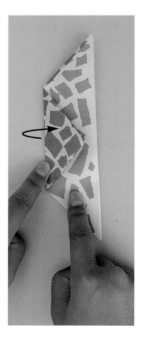

8 Open out the last fold and make a triangle fold by lifting up the top flap and flattening it into a triangle.

9 Turn over the paper and lift the square flap before opening it up and pressing it down again as a triangle.

10 Spin the paper 180° and fold the triangle's tip over to meet the long edge.

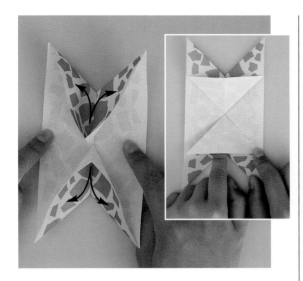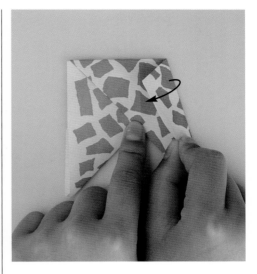

11 Placing your fingers inside the object, open it out before flattening it again, folding over the tips from the inside to make a square.

12 Fold the object in half.

13 Take the top right corner and fold it forward so that the outer edge runs along the edge of the long point.

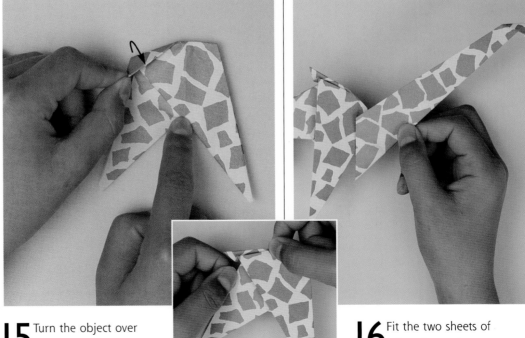

14 Fold the back leg in half and turn the crease inside the object.

15 Turn the object over and turn over the top corner before folding it inside the object to make the tail.

16 Fit the two sheets of origami together to complete the giraffe.

19 **KAERU** FROG

This little frog jumps when you push down on its back legs lightly with a finger. A simple design, you can make it with a group of friends, and have fun competing to see whose frog jumps highest. This is one of the most traditional origami models, dating from the days when there were not many toys for children to play with, and they had to make their own amusements.

• • • • • • • • • • • • • • • • • •
You will need
6 in (15 cm) sheet of stiff, green paper

| Fold the paper in half, then open it out and repeat in the other direction before folding all the corners into the center.

2 Spin the paper through 45°, turn in the outer points so that the edges run down the center line, and then fold up the bottom to make a triangle.

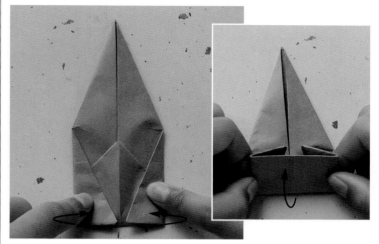

3 Turn in the bottom corners to the center line and fold the bottom up to the line where the corner flaps cross the lifted flap to make a crease.

4 Fold the flap made in step 3 in half, bringing the end back down toward you.

5 Fold the tip forward to make the head then let the object stand up. Push the back and watch it hop.

20 USHI COW

Making animals with specially-patterned paper is very popular in Japan: this spotted paper is perfect for a cow. Use one sheet for the neck and head, and a second for the legs and body, joining them together with glue. Alternatively, paint patterns on to white paper—your cow will be the only one like it in the world!

You will need
2 sheets of 6 in (15 cm) square paper
Paper glue

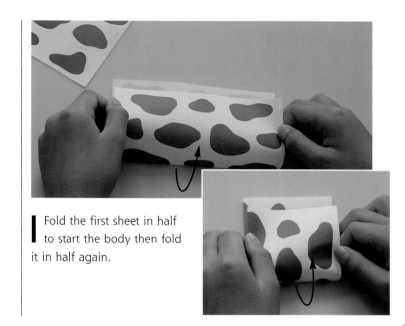

1 Fold the first sheet in half to start the body then fold it in half again.

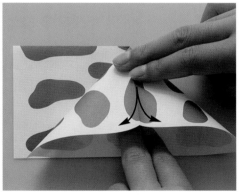

2 Open out the top flap and refold into a triangle before turning the object over and repeating on the other side.

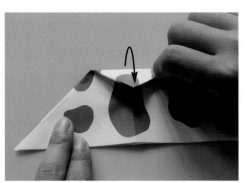

3 Turn the tip forward, folding it so that the point reaches halfway down the body.

4 Placing your fingers inside, pull the sheets apart to open them out and flatten, making triangles at both ends.

75

USHI COW

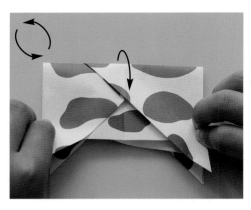

5 Spin the object 90° and fold the back forward along the middle crease.

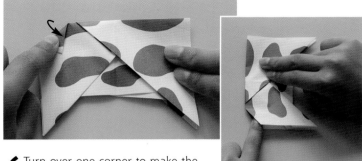

6 Turn over one corner to make the rear of the body and fold it back inside.

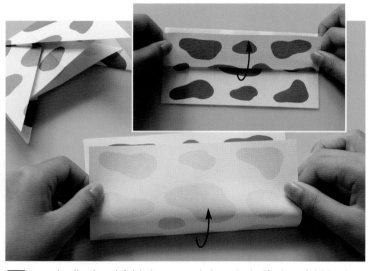

7 To make the head fold the second sheet in half, then fold both edges back up to the first fold line.

8 Fold the corner made up of two folded sheets up to the other edge of the object to make a crease.

9 Unfold the crease and open out the top fold, pressing it down into a triangle.

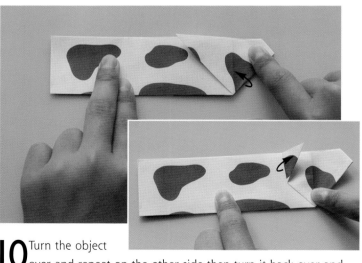

10 Turn the object over and repeat on the other side then turn it back over and press the end point underneath to make the nose. Next, fold the triangle's other point forward to make an ear and repeat on the back.

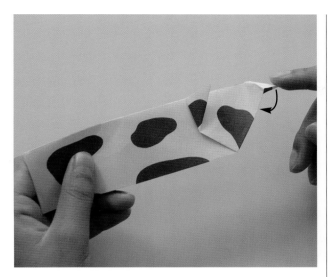

11 Turn the nose inside out and press back inside the object.

12 Fold the neck at an angle, starting underneath the ear.

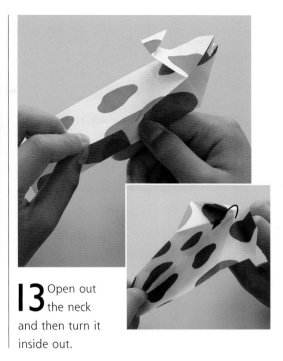

13 Open out the neck and then turn it inside out.

14 Refold along the angled crease.

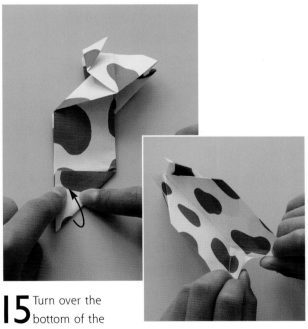

15 Turn over the bottom of the neck at an angle then turn it inside out and press it back inside the neck.

16 Fix the two pieces together with glue.

21 KASANE-BAKO
STACK OF BOXES

Use multi-colored paper to make a stack of boxes, each one smaller than the last so that each fits inside the next. Each box is simple to create from just a single sheet of paper, with origami techniques that use neither scissors nor glue. If you want to make a lid for each of the boxes just use two sheets of each color, one a fraction larger than the other so that it will fit as a lid when folded in the same way.

You will need
10 sheets of different-colored paper

1 Take 10 pieces of paper and cut down nine of them so that each is ¹/₂ in (1 cm) shorter and narrower than the last.

2 Make the largest box first. To start, fold the sheet in half, open it out, fold in the other direction, turn over, and fold the corners into the center.

3 Fold the edges into the middle then spin the paper through 90° and turn in the narrow ends to make a square.

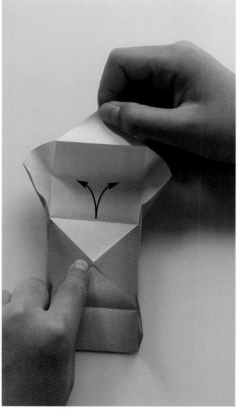

4 Open the paper all the way out and pull up one flap, then repeat on the opposite flap.

5 Turn over the creases at the sides of the flap and press them together to make the solid corners.

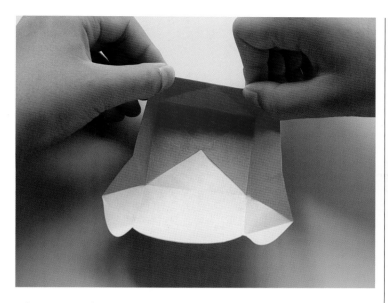

6 Turn over the creases at the sides of the flap and press them together to make the solid corners.

7 Repeat at the other end to complete the box.

8 Make up the other nine boxes from the smaller sheets in exactly the same way.

TIP

Choose the brightest colors you can find to create the best effect when the boxes are placed inside each other. Rainbow colors are a good starting point: Red, orange, yellow, green, blue, indigo, and violet. Then add in any other colors you like.

KASANE-BAKO STACK OF BOXES

22 SAN-POU CANDY BOX

This traditional origami design is perfect for holding little treats. For a birthday party, make original gift boxes in a range of patterned paper for all the guests to take home. This candy box is small enough to fit in the hand but you could make one in any size or even stick a plain piece of paper on to the back of the *edo-chiyogami* to make an interesting contrast.

You will need
1 sheet of *edo-chiyogami* 8 x 8 in (20 x 20 cm)

Fold the piece of *edo-chiyogami* in half then open it out and repeat after turning the sheet through 90° to make two creases.

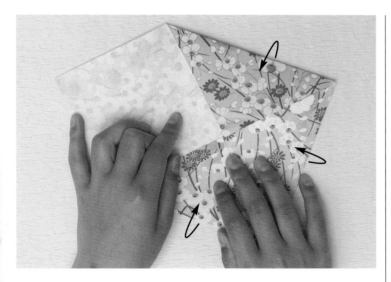

2 Bring all four corners into the center to leave the paper in the "floor cushion" shape.

3 Fold the paper back on itself with a mountain fold and then fold in half from right to left to make a valley fold.

SAN-POU CANDY BOX

4 Put your fingers inside the top fold and pull up. The pocket will open out and the left-hand corner will rise. Press this point down on what was the top of the triangle, making a diamond shape.

5 Turn the paper over and repeat the previous step, pulling up the large flap and folding the corner down to the top of the diamond.

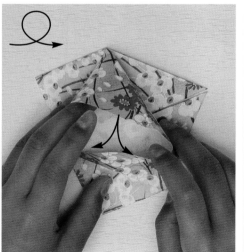

6 Spin the paper through 90° then place your fingers inside the opening as far as they will go. Open the flaps together and fold the paper down away from you into a rectangle.

7 Turn the paper over and open out the other flaps, folding them flat so that the paper is left in the shape of a simple house.

8 Turn over one of the flaps on both the front and back of the object to leave both faces showing no folds.

9 Lift the top flaps on both the left and the right and fold them so that they meet in the center of the object.

10 Turn the object over and repeat on the reverse.

11 Fold over flaps on both the front and reverse of the object to leave both faces showing no folds then turn up the bottom by about 1 1/4 in (3 cm) to make a crease.

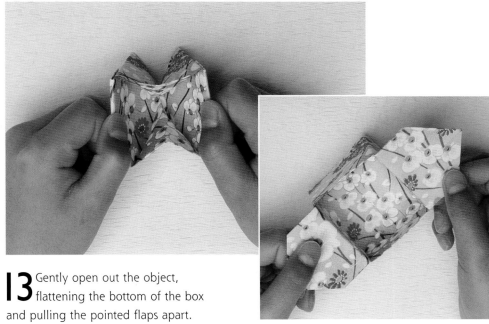

12 Fold the pointed ends over the main body of the object.

13 Gently open out the object, flattening the bottom of the box and pulling the pointed flaps apart.

23 **NAPUKIN RINGU**
NAPKIN RING

Long, narrow strips of papers in two contrasting colors make a napkin ring that creates a vivid impression of alternating shades. You can lengthen the ring with extra strips of each color to transform it into a bracelet. You can also enjoy making sets of colored rings, which look great together. Try linking some rings to form a paper necklace.

You will need
3 strips of red and 3 strips of purple paper
Paper glue

1 Cut two pieces of origami into strips and place the ends of one of each color on top of each other at 90°.

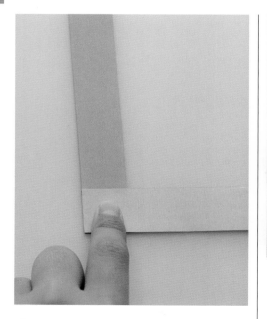

2 Turn each end over the other so that the backs of the strips are showing.

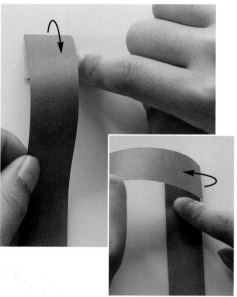

3 Continue to turn each end over the other as above.

4 Join the next length of paper by sticking the dark side against the light side of the same color with glue.

86

PARTY TIME

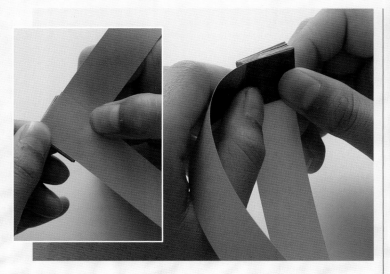 

5 Repeat with the second color, again sticking the dark side to the light, and continue folding.

6 Add the third strip in the same way and finish by joining one end to the other: place glue on the light purple end and stick it to the other light purple end and repeat with the pink strip.

24 COP-SHIKI COASTER

This wonderful coaster is made with modern, flower-patterned origami paper. This design is finished neatly when you take out crease lines properly. Use exactly the same folding method to make an origami medal, simply folding the four corners to the reverse side after the last step. Both the medal and the coaster will be very popular at a party.

You will need
6 in (15 cm) sheet of brightly colored paper

I Fold the sheet in half to make a crease, then fold both sides into the center so that the edges meet along the crease.

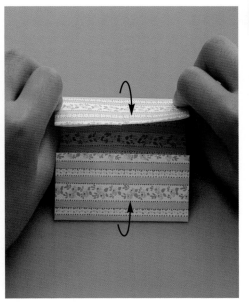

2 Turn the paper over and fold in the sides so that they meet at the center.

COP-SHIKI COASTER

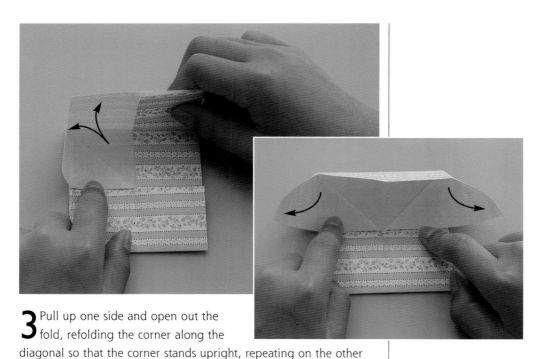

TIP

Make sure that your folds are accurate and as sharp as possible, so take your time—don't rush it. Remember to work at a table so you can press down firmly on folds. It's also much easier than holding the paper in mid-air.

3 Pull up one side and open out the fold, refolding the corner along the diagonal so that the corner stands upright, repeating on the other side of the same flap.

4 Repeat the previous step on the other flap then press them down flat, making pointed ends.

5 Pick up the top left flap and fold upward, then fold out the other three flaps in the same way.

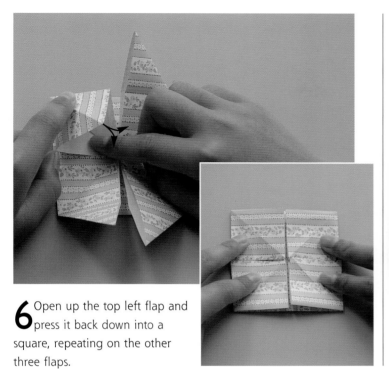

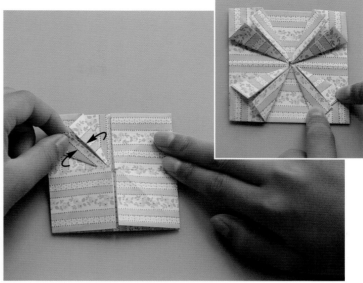

6 Open up the top left flap and press it back down into a square, repeating on the other three flaps.

7 Turn in the corners of each of the four squares so that the edges meet in the middle along the line between the opposite corners.

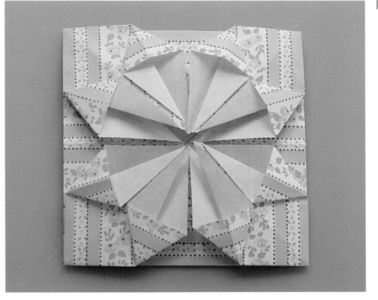

8 Pull up each of the small flaps just created, opening them out before pressing them down again, making small triangles at the top of each.

9 Repeat until all the flaps have been opened to make a circle of plain color in the center of the coaster.

25 **KAMI-COP** CUP

Difficulty rating ● ○ ○

This paper cup, which is very easy to make, works best when made with paper which has color on both the front and back. Ideally, make it with stiff paper or so it can stand up when you press down the base. The same design made with a large piece of square paper makes a fun paper hat if it is turned upside down.

You will need

1 sheet of 8 in (20 cm) square drawing paper, colored on both sides

1 Fold the paper from corner to corner.

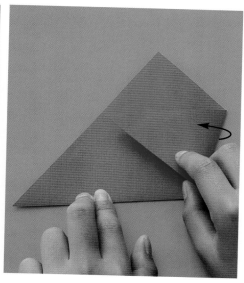

2 Fold the bottom corner across to the middle of the opposite edge so that the top edge is horizontal.

3 Turn the front of the top flap over the flat edge.

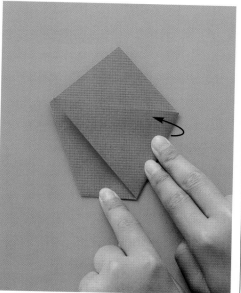

4 Turn the paper over and take the remaining point across to the angle on the other edge.

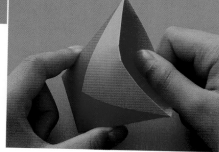

5 Fold forward the other top point. Put your fingers inside the object and open out the cup.

26 HANA-KAGO FLOWER BASKET

A small flower basket, made with beautiful, flower-patterned origami becomes a cute decoration or candy case at a girls' party—make one out of different paper for every guest. Or you can make a genuine flower basket from a large sheet of strong drawing paper.

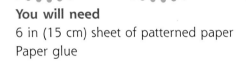

You will need
6 in (15 cm) sheet of patterned paper
Paper glue

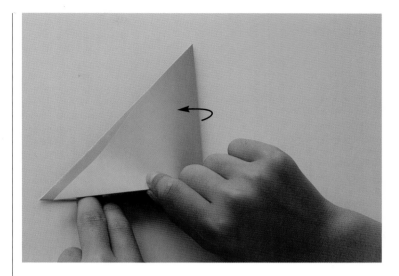

Holding down the sheet on the left side as shown, fold the sheet corner to corner and fold it in half again.

2 Pull up the top flap and reflatten to make a square fold and repeat on the other side.

3 Turn over the top flap to make a crease.

4 Fold the tip of the flap into the center and then fold flat the flap. Repeat on the reverse of the object.

5 From the top-left corner, turn the top flap down to the bottom right. Turn the object over and repeat on the back.

TIP

This project does take a little time to perfect, but as you get to do every type of fold on the front and the reverse of the basket, you get more practice as you go!

6 Turn the top flap into the center from the top left-hand corner so that the edge runs along the diagonal center line. Now bring the bottom right-hand corner into the center in the same way. Turn the object over and repeat.

7 Open up the flaps turning the top corner in so that the upper edge of the flap runs down the left-hand crease. Repeat on the bottom corner so that the right-hand edge runs along the right-hand crease.

8 Fold both flaps back over then turn the object over and repeat from step 6 on the reverse.

9 Fold the wide end across to make a crease between the side flaps.

10 Placing your fingers inside the object, gently open out the basket, ensuring that all the corners remain intact.

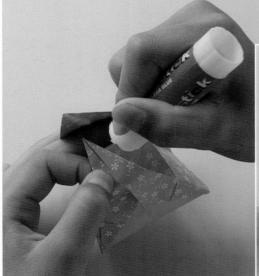

11 Use paper glue to join the two long ends together to make the basket's handle, pressing them together to make a solid join.

27 MILLEFEUILLE CAKE

Millefeuille is a very popular cake throughout Japan even though it has its origins in France, which gave it its name, meaning "1,000 pieces of leaves." There are specially printed origami papers for candies and cakes that imitate the real thing when complete. If you can't find the special paper, you can draw or paint the design on plain paper, using the pattern opposite as a guide.

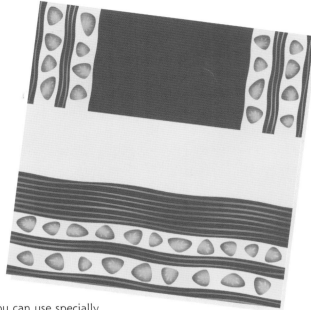

You will need
2 sheets of 6 in (15 cm) specially printed paper for each slice
3 in (7.5 cm) square of paper for the decoration

You can use specially printed origami to make the main slice of cake. Alternatively, decorate your own sheet of plain paper and follow the instructions below.

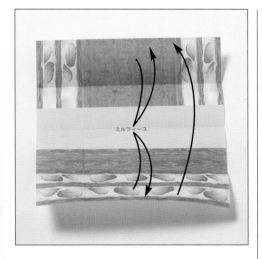

1 Fold the edges of the sheet so that they meet in the center, making two creases, then open out the paper and fold it in half.

2 Fold the sides of the sheet into the center, then open them out again to leave two creases.

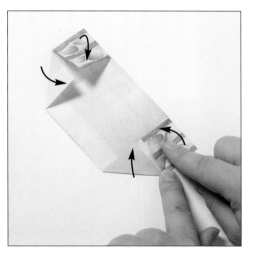

3 Fold the bottom corners up at a 45° angle, then turn over the top flaps at the upper corners to meet the bottom corners along the center line.

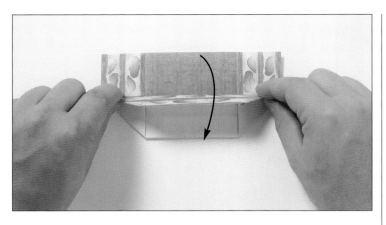

4 Turn down the top flap, folding it along the central crease so that the top edge rests on the bottom of the paper.

5 Turn the paper over, ensuring that you are left with a completely flat surface.

6 Fold back the top corners, bringing them down to the center line before releasing them to leave diagonal creases.

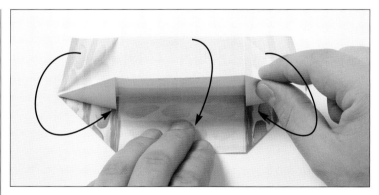

7 Fold forward the top half of the paper and, lifting the bottom flap slightly, tuck the corners inside the folds.

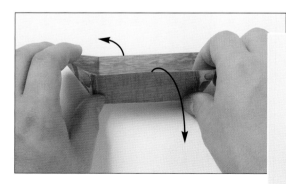

8 Gently open out the paper, pressing the ends straight, so that the two large faces are at right angles to each other.

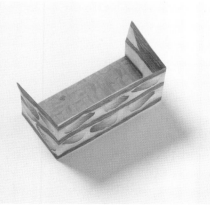

9 Make a second piece and slot the two together to complete the slice of cake.

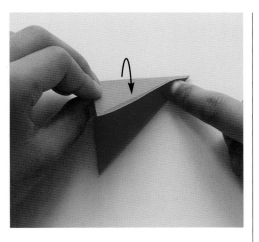

10 To make the decoration, take the square origami and fold it from corner to corner and then in half.

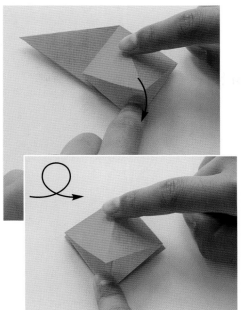

11 Lift one of the triangular flaps and fold back as a square, turning over and repeating on the back.

12 Turn up the top flap and press it back down by folding it over itself.

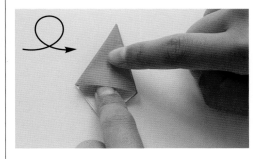

13 Turn the object over and repeat on the back, lifting and refolding the top flap.

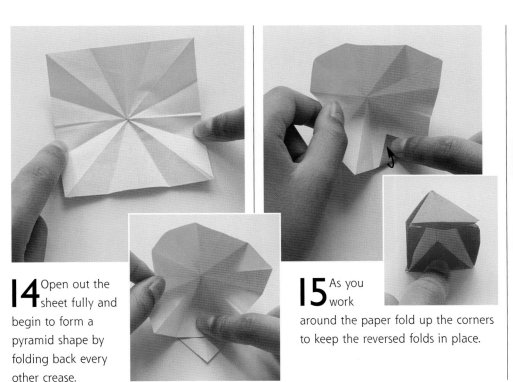

14 Open out the sheet fully and begin to form a pyramid shape by folding back every other crease.

15 As you work around the paper fold up the corners to keep the reversed folds in place.

16 Form the base from two sheets of origami and place the pyramid on top when they are joined together.

28 CHOCOLATE CAKE

A chocolate cake is always popular, and it is so easy to make this creamy treat that looks good enough to eat. The design transforms itself into other cakes when you change the color of the base: using yellow origami makes a very lifelike cheesecake. You can create an entire array of delights for your very own bakery.

You will need
2 paper rectangles 6 x 3 in (15 x 7.5 cm)
2 sheets of 3 in (7.5 cm) square paper
Paper ribbon
Paper glue
Scissors

Make two rectangular pieces of origami and two small squares, with the same dimension as the short sides of the rectangles.

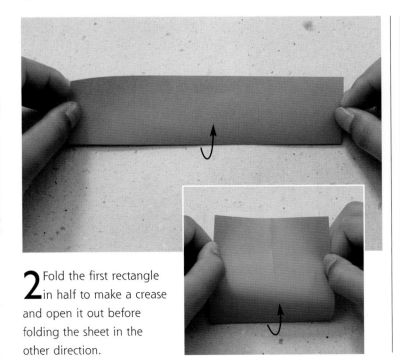

2 Fold the first rectangle in half to make a crease and open it out before folding the sheet in the other direction.

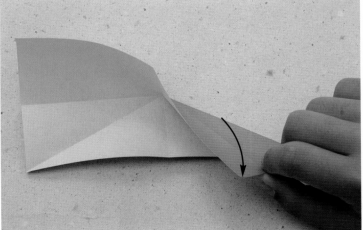

3 Now make diagonal creases by folding the paper from corner to corner, taking care to run the crease through the center point of the paper.

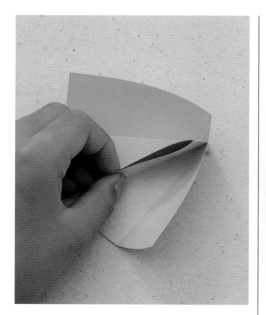

4 Taking both ends of the same long edge, pinch them together so that the paper turns on itself across half of the horizontal crease.

5 Fold the inside flap in half and press it down against the flat area of the paper to hold the object together.

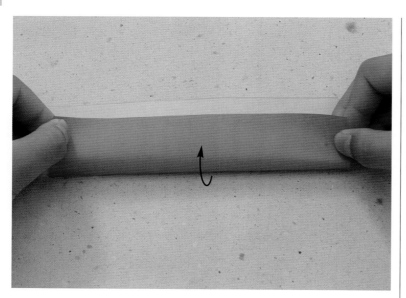

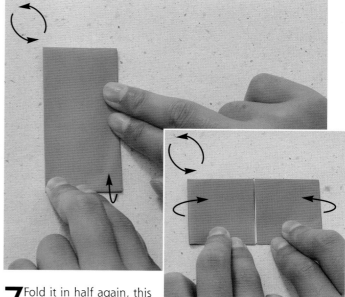

6 Take the second rectangular sheet and fold it in half.

7 Fold it in half again, this time across its width then open it out and fold the ends in to meet in the center.

8 Let the folds open out and push the second sheet of origami into the opening of the first piece of origami.

9 Hold them together by gluing a strip of patterned paper or origami ribbon all the way around the cake, using paper glue.

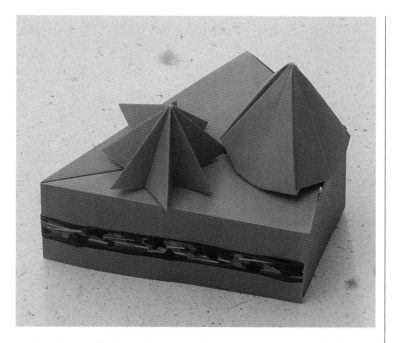

10 Make small decorations from the two square pieces of origami and place them on top (see page 101).

29 SANDWICH

This delicious-looking sandwich is made using special paper that recreates the look of toasted bread. You could make up an entire tea party with different fillings, from fried eggs and bacon to healthy salad! If you prefer, draw a picture of some toast on white paper to look like this origami paper and also cut out your favorite fillings as you make them.

You will need
2 pieces of 6 in (15 cm) specially-printed paper for each slice
Origami decorations

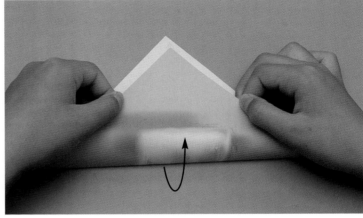

I Fold the first sheet from corner to corner to make a crease, then open out and repeat, folding across the opposite corners.

2 Open the sheet out again and fold all the corners into the center, making a square.

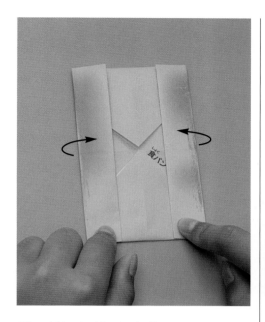

3 Fold both sides in, halfway to the center of the object.

4 Fold down the ends, again halfway to the center.

5 Open out the ends of the object and reverse the corners at the bottom of each flap so that they will fold down into solid corners with the sides.

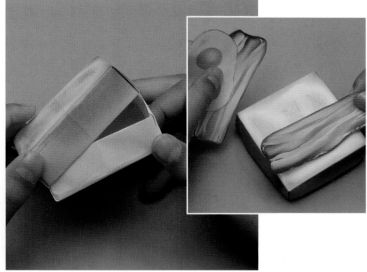

6 Repeat at the other end to make a solid box base.

7 Repeat with a second sheet of origami, then fit them together to make one slice of toast and add some decorations.

30 HOT DOG

Test your origami skills with this hot dog. You can use brown origami paper for the bread, and make the sausage using a rectangular sheet of paper. The bread is made from a whole sheet of origami and can seem a little tricky at first, but don't worry because the sausage is easy.

You will need
6 x 3 in (15 x 7.5 cm) sheet of specially patterned paper
6 in (15cm) square of brown paper

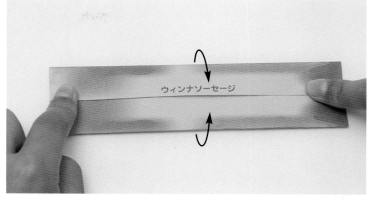

I To make the sausage, take the rectangular sheet and fold it in half to make a crease. Open it out and fold both edges into the center to run together along the crease.

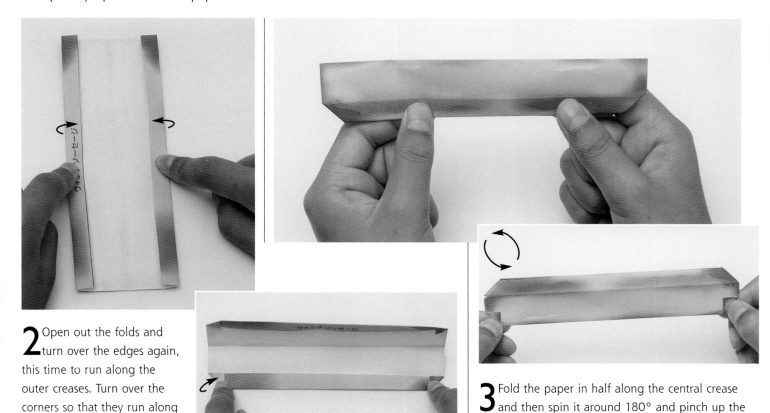

2 Open out the folds and turn over the edges again, this time to run along the outer creases. Turn over the corners so that they run along the edges of the folds.

3 Fold the paper in half along the central crease and then spin it around 180° and pinch up the folded corners.

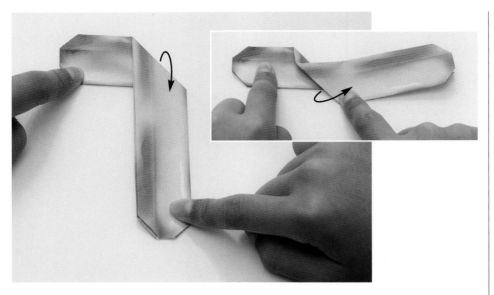

4 Give the sausage texture by folding it with a 45° angle about 1½ in (4 cm) from one end, then take the folded end back with a second angled fold ½ in (1 cm) further along.

5 Repeat the angled folds three more times along the object then stretch it open to reveal the concertina effect.

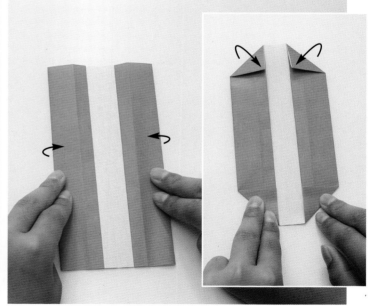

6 To make the bun take the second sheet and fold it in half. Then bring the sides into the center before opening again and turning the edges over about ½ in (1 cm).

7 Fold the sides into the center using the original creases, leaving a ¾ in (2 cm) gap in the middle, then turn over the corners at an angle to the edge of the turn.

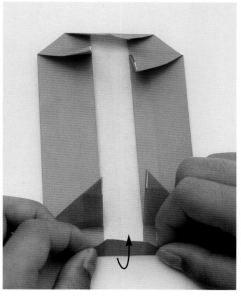

8 Lift up each corner, opening out and reversing them, refolding each one inside the flap, leaving the same shape as before.

9 Raise the four triangle flaps you have just made and fold up the remaining end by 1/2 in (1 cm).

10 Lift these little flaps at the sides and fold them back so that they can slip underneath the raised triangle flaps, their folds reversing.

11 Fold down the raised triangles, tweaking the ends into creases.

12 Slip the sausage into position, holding it in place with the four turned corners.

31 PIZZA

Think about your favorite pizza toppings and recreate them on your very own
paper pizza, making eight similar segments to complete each one. Start the pizza
party by making origami together before you eat the real thing!

You will need
2 sheets of 6 in (15 cm) specially printed paper cut into quarters to make 8 squares

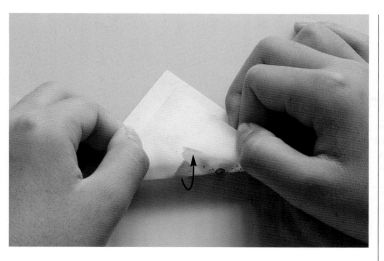

1 Cut two pieces of origami into quarters and take the first one, folding it from corner to corner to make a crease.

2 Open out the sheet of paper and fold the bottom corner up to the center crease so that the bottom edge of the paper now runs down the crease. Repeat with the top corner.

3 Fold the wide end over the ends of the two flaps.

4 Turn the paper over and fold up about ¼ in (½ cm) to make the pizza crust.

5 Repeat the same steps to make the other seven segments of the pizza.

32 KO-BUNE BOAT

This origami boat is one of the traditional origami models and uses some of the folding methods common to other projects in this book—origami techniques become steadily simpler as you practice them! A boat has always been a popular toy and this one is so easy to make that very soon you will create a small fleet of your own.

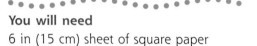

You will need
6 in (15 cm) sheet of square paper

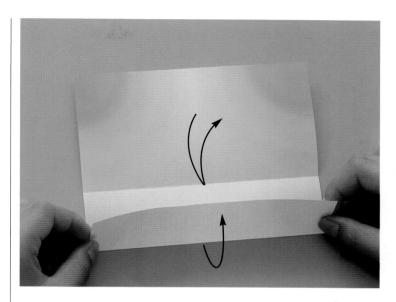

1 Fold the origami in half to make a crease and open out, then fold the bottom edge up to the center line.

KO-BUNE BOAT

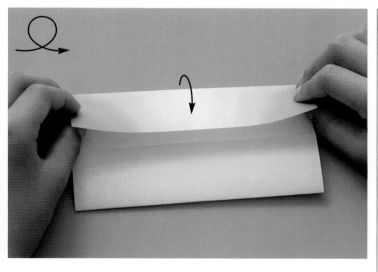

2 Turn over and fold the top half down to the middle.

3 Spin the paper through 180° and then turn the left-hand flap over, folding the paper in half to make a crease.

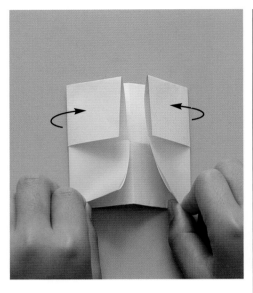

4 Open out and fold both edges into the center line.

5 Open out the top of the left-hand flap, flattening it into a triangle fold and repeat on the right-hand side.

6 Open out the left-hand side and pull open the bottom flap, flattening it to make a triangle.

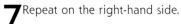

7 Repeat on the right-hand side.

If you don't have origami paper or a strong paper to hand, and you have to use thin, more delicate paper, be gentle when pulling out the lower half of the boat in Step 9. When finished, the boat will be more resilient than during construction, so take care not to damage the paper as you work.

8 Turn the bottom left-hand triangle up and fold it across to the left, repeating on the right.

9 Pull open the lower half of the object and fold the top half down into the opening.

10 Finish by opening out the boat.

33 **HIKOUKI** AIRPLANE

Making paper darts has been a children's favorite for many years. Now take to the air with this simple but effective origami design. Use any kind of origami paper and then just launch the plane into the sky. You can make this airplane in no time at all, and if you do it carefully it will fly surprisingly well.

You will need
6 in (15 cm) sheet of square paper

Fold the origami in half to make a crease.

2 Open out the paper and fold the corners from one side down to the center line.

3 Fold one side into the center again to form the wing.

4 Repeat on the other side to make the second wing, then fold back the tip to make the snub nose.

118

VEHICLES

5 Fold the object in half ensuring the folded nose is on the outside.

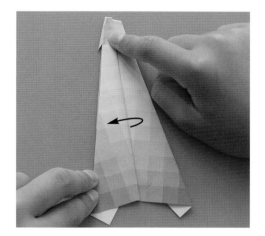

6 Fold down one wing.

7 Repeat on the second wing and open out the airplane.

34 ROKETTO ROCKET

Fly into space with this simple rocket made from a metal-colored origami paper. Using silver paper is especially successful if it has a contrasting color on the reverse side. If you like, you can use white paper to make the rocket then get some coloring pens and decorate it with your own unique design. Let your imagination take off!

You will need
6 in (15 cm) sheet of square metallic paper for each rocket

Fold the sheet of origami in half and then into quarters.

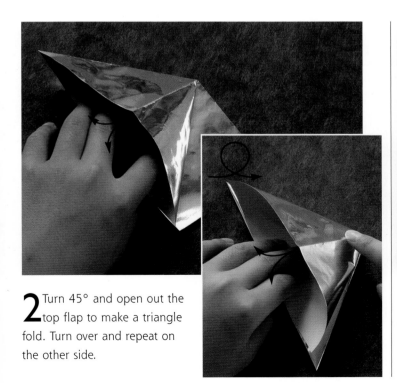

2 Turn 45° and open out the top flap to make a triangle fold. Turn over and repeat on the other side.

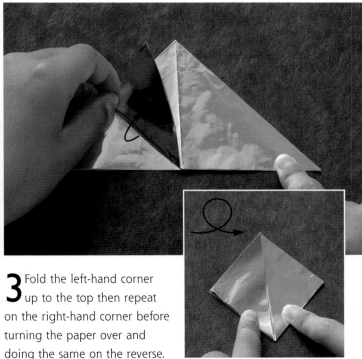

3 Fold the left-hand corner up to the top then repeat on the right-hand corner before turning the paper over and doing the same on the reverse.

4 Open up the left-hand flap and press down into a square, repeating on the right-hand side and the reverse.

5 Open up the left-hand flap and press down into a square, repeating on the right-hand side and the reverse.

6 Turn the top flap on the left over to the right, leaving the paper with a plain surface. Repeat on the back.

7 Fold both sides into the center then turn over and repeat.

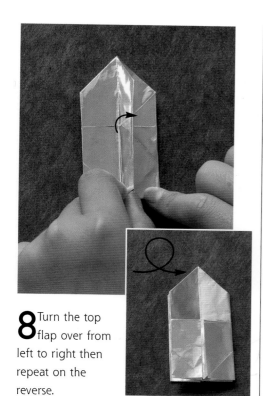

8 Turn the top flap over from left to right then repeat on the reverse.

9 Pull up the right-hand square flap, opening it out and flattening it into a triangle before repeating on the left-hand side.

10 Turn the object over and repeat the previous step.

11 To finish, open out the folds. If you want to make a space shuttle instead of a rocket, hold two of the flaps together to leave two wings.

35 YOTTO YACHT

For this yacht I used paper that has contrasting colors on both sides, but any kind of paper will work equally well, and it's easy to make whatever age you are. Let the yacht sail away with the origami boat (see pages 114–117) and make a flotilla in any color or size you like.

You will need
10 in (25 cm) sheet of square colored drawing paper

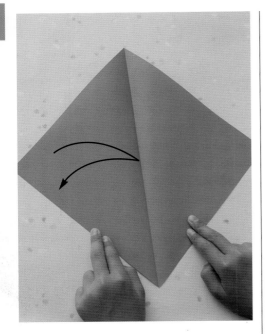

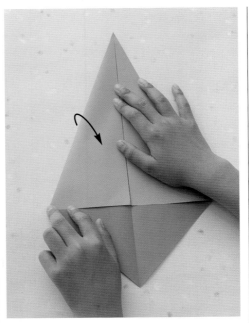

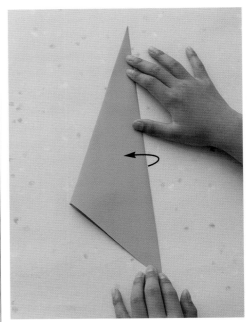

1 Fold the sheet of paper corner to corner and open out.	**2** Fold the corners into the center line so that the edges runs vertically along the crease.	**3** Fold the object in half.

124

VEHICLES

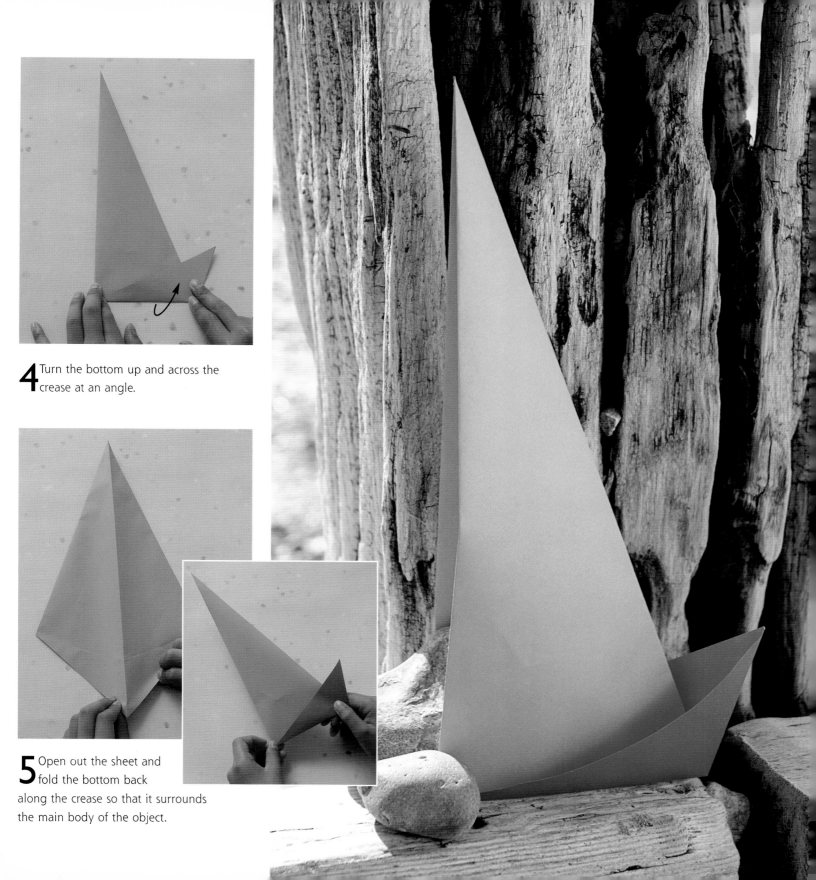

4 Turn the bottom up and across the crease at an angle.

5 Open out the sheet and fold the bottom back along the crease so that it surrounds the main body of the object.

USEFUL INFORMATION

SUPPLIERS

JAPAN
Showa Grimm Co.,Ltd
www.showa-grimm.co.jp

USA
JP Trading,INC.
800 Burlway Road Unit #A, Burlingame, Ca 94010
Tel: 650-340-6130
www.jptrading.com
E-mail: info@jptrading.com

Hakubundo,Inc.
1600 Kapiolani Blvd. Suite 121, Honolulu, Hawaii 96814
Tel: 808-947-5503
www.hakubundo.com
E-mail: hakubundo@hakubundo.com

J Kids Square
PO Box 5821, Bellevue, WA 98006, USA
Tel: 425-765-4540 / 888-834-4485
www.jkidssquare.com (online shop Japanese only)

www.origamisources.com
Useful resource for origami stockists in the US

UK
Jp-Books (Uk) Ltd.
C/o Mitsukoshi, Dorland House, 14-20 Regent Street,
London SW1Y 4PH
Tel: 020 7839 4839
E-mail: info@jpbooks.co.uk

Japan Centre
212 Piccadilly, London W1J 9HX
Tel: 020 7439 8035
www.japancentre.com

Hobbycraft
Tel: 0800 027 2387
www.hobbycraft.co.uk

FRANCE
Culture Japon S.A.S.
Maison du la culture du Japon
101 Bis. Quai Branly 75015, Paris
Tel: 01 45 79 02 00
E-mail: culturejpt@wanadoo.fr

BOOKS

The Simple Art of Japanese Papercrafts, Mari Ono (Cico Books)
Fun with Origami, Kazuo Kobayashi (Kodansha International Ltd.)

WEBSITES

British Origami Society www.britishorigami.info

Japan Origami Academic Society www.origami.gr.jp

Nippon Origami Association www.origami-noa.com

Origami Club www.origami-club.com/en

Origami Instructions www.origami-instructions.com

INDEX

ACKNOWLEDGMENTS

The publication of this book could not have been achieved without all the generous help and co-operation given by family, friends and many others.

My special thanks go to Cindy Richards, Robin Gurdon, Sally Powell and Pete Jorgensen of Cico Books; Debbie Patterson and Carolyn Barber for taking the photographs; Claire Legemah for designing this book; and all others who were involved in its publication.

Thanks also to Mr Yukio Taguchi at Showa Grimm Co.,Ltd. in Japan for his sincere cooperation; to Yoko Moon and her children for acting as models; to Ben Rogers for proofreading; and finally to my son Roshin, for acting as the model for all the projects, for translating my draft and all his other support.

I also want to thank all the readers of this book who become interested in origami and Japanese culture.

My special thanks to the origami artists and creators who consented to the inclusion of their original designs in this book: Dokuhotei Nakano: 26, 28, 66, 74; Isamu Asahi: 70, 73, 76, 80, 83, 86